The Secr
of Us Kids

— • — • —

A
CHILDHOOD
MEMOIR
1941-1945

— • — • —

by award-winning author
Bonnie Buckley Maldonado
in collaboration with Patrick F. Buckley III

an seanchai imprint

This book is dedicated to all the children,
then and now, who endure hard times.

An Seanchai Imprint
23 Oxbow Dr., Silver City, NM 88061
bonniemusing@gmail.com

ISBN 10: 1-59152-149-1
ISBN 13: 978-1-59152-149-5

Front cover: Childhood Diary of Bonnie Mae Buckley, 1941-42.
Back cover: Derrick, Border Field, 1930

For more information, write contact Farcountry Press, PO Box 5630,
Helena, MT 59602; 1-800-821-3874.

You may order extra copies of this book by calling Farcountry Press
toll free at (800) 821-3874.

sweetgrassbooks
a division of Farcountry Press

Produced by Sweetgrass Books.
PO Box 5630, Helena, MT 59604; (800) 821-3874; www.sweetgrassbooks.com.

The views expressed by the author/publisher in this book do not necessarily represent
the views of, nor should be attributed to, Sweetgrass Books. Sweetgrass Books is not
responsible for the content of the author/publisher's work.

Produced and printed in the United States of America.

18   17   16   15   14   1   2   3   4   5

Table of Contents

THE LONGEST SEASON

WHEN THE CROCUSES BLOOM

Introduction

This is no fairy tale childhood or ghost story though
I could dig up ghosts like my great aunt Anna dug up
her recently dead twelve-year-old, fearing her to have
been buried alive.

This memoir has to do with my dream of my mother
yelling, "You can't publish that old stuff. You know
it is not to be told." I hollered back, "I have lived a
long life with the darkness. It is time to set it free."
It is our story, the kids' story, even though Mama's
story wants to take over. It is a story of how four chil-
dren reacted to the losses around them. It expresses
doubts about our family being able to hold together.
We survived the Great Depression, but would we
make it past the first year of World War II?

My brother Pat and I were in our late seventies, driving
down Highway 287 between Augusta and Choteau,
Montana. I asked him what came to mind when he
thought about our growing up in the Border Field.
"We sure as hell came up short when it came to being
kids," he responded. I felt tears in my eyes. There he
was in his old straw hat, driving his Chevy with the
worn vinyl top, and me with white hair, both awash
with old insecurities all over again. He was twelve,
doing Dad's job, his arms and face smeared with crude
oil after cleaning the inside of an oil tank. I was ten and
making biscuits which wouldn't turn out very well.

Our family landed in the oilfield two miles from the
family ranch, which was lost to the bank in 1937. We
were marooned seven miles west of Sweet Grass on
the Alberta-Montana border. Dad had taken a job as
a pumper and refinery worker in the Border Field.
A shack of a house was thrown in with Daddy's

salary of one hundred and twenty a month. Gone
was the safety net of an extended family on an idyllic
Victorian ranch sequestered in a coulee that had been
our spiritual home. Boundaries were blurred in the oil-
field. We did what we knew to keep things going when
my mother left to maintain her sanity, and Dad was out
delivering gas and stove oil many miles from us.

The oilfield was a rough and unpredictable place, shared
with refugees of the Dust Bowl. Our parents seemed
unable to recover from their losses. Alcohol became our
father's escape. Our mother's many talents were dimmed
by depression so severe that she would become suicidal.

Neighbors and people from town were oblivious to
our problems. "Look at you doing so well," we heard.
Looking good. We were good at that. We knew better
than to tell that our mother might kill herself or leave
forever. We knew Dad would come home if the tanker
truck didn't wreck because he was drinking. A refinery
worker dropped a timber on our little dog, Blackie.
It made us aware of how easy it is to be smashed. We
played on the ice, steering our sleds over treacherous
pipelines and perilous slopes of uncertainty unaware
of where or how we might end up.

The reader will hear the voices of children living in
a time that no longer exists, in a world long forgotten.
The poems contain the lines of a childhood diary, and
the memories encrypted in our hearts—the smell of
wild grasses after a rain, the sight of oil leaking onto
new grass, the worries about money, about our parents.

Is memory accurate? Are words written down to be
trusted? Only the reader can decide.

Acknowledgments

My thanks to Kathy Springmeyer, of Farcountry Press
for suggesting that I write a childhood memoir.

I could not have written *The Secret Lives of Us Kids*
without the contributions of my brothers, Pat, Mike
and Jerry Buckley.

The invaluable editing support of Larry and Elvira
Godfrey, and JJ Wilson.

George and Malinda Austin of Silver Imaging for scan-
ning, cropping and enlarging many tiny, fragile photos.

Boisvert Photography of Sunburst, Montana for the
archival photograph of Sweet Grass.

Joseph Silva, grandson for his idea of featuring my
old diary on the cover.

JW Mcpherson Society for the Arts for love, support
and suggestions through the past year.

Miller Library, Western New Mexico University.

My husband, Librado, for being the best listener
and supporter of all.

So Short the Summer

The Car Burnt Up

She drove that 1938 Chevrolet
over two ruts
with high prairie grass between
to Jim Baker's turn-off
where she set that car on fire,
hardly saving herself.

Angry at Daddy
for wrecking the car
when he hit a pig
driving drunk,
she took action.

She would not endure again
the sound of the front wheels
scraping the fenders
like so many fingernails
irritating a blackboard.

She poured a can of gas
over the backseat
and tossed a kitchen match.

The flames roared and jumped
inside and out,
singeing her long dark hair
and burning off her eyelashes.

She walked home in shock
smelling like gas and fire
and hysterics.

Daddy rushed to her
telling us kids
to stay outside.
We didn't wait.

Racing over the prairie
like anxious coyotes
we followed the smoke
to find the burning car.

Mama is worse than a kid
sparking a flame
for a prairie fire.
But she is smart,
waits until it rains.

The insurance agent
accepted their account.
They have two-hundred dollars
for another car.

Pat, Mike, Jerry and Bonnie Buckley

Us Kids

There are four.
Pat has black hair
like Daddy.
Black Irish some say.
He is curious
and so happy
to find how things work.
He is twelve.

I am the girl,
two years younger.
I am told I am nice.
My grades are mostly "A's."

Mike came with red hair.
He is a smart, sweet boy,
only eight and worries so.
"Sensitive." my mother says.

Jerry is six.
He has a warrior's eyes.
He says things like
"Our cat is Gray Cat.
She is gray."
He gave Joe, the canary,
a bath, and Joe expired
in the suds.

We play together
when there is time.
Living here is not so bad
with each other.

The Border Field

Miss Hiely told us to write
about where we live.
"Paint a picture in words."

We play in "No-Man's Land"
between Canada and the U.S.
Our house is one-fourth mile
from Canada.

There are shady coulees
where wild flowers grow,
and chokecherries
stain our hands purple
in September.

There are sand rocks
like castles, caves,
and the Buffalo Jump
with many arrowheads.
It used to be our land.

Badgers dig holes,
and coyotes howl
at shooting stars.
Crocuses hide
beneath prairie grasses,
and gophers stand straight
as tin soldiers.

The Rocky Mountains
are snow-capped in summer.
They and the Blackfeet Reservation
are west of us.

Russian thistles hide fence lines,
and tumbleweeds
hug the barbed wire.
Oil flows
over sweet grass.
Ducks land on sumps,
thinking they are water.
They die covered
with thick, black oil.

We go to sleep and awake
to the sounds of pump jacks.
There are derricks
and noisy flywheels
where sheep once grazed.

Daddy pumps oil wells
and runs a refinery
for Mr. Banana.
He is curved like one,
with a lardy stomach
above bandy little legs.
He throws back his head
and blows cigar smoke
in our direction.

"Talk about sleazy,"
Mama mumbles.
She knows Daddy isn't paid
what he is worth.
Daddy's work is perfect
because that is how he is.

Our house has four rooms,
a store room and a cellar.
I would like the storeroom
for my own, but I can't ask.

Mama hems white curtains
on the Singer treadle.
She Kalsomines dirty walls
in different colors
to make it homier.

Beth's oil painting
of a bear on a cliff
scares me at night.
He likes to stare
into my eyes.

Our bedroom is crowded
with bunk beds
made from 2X4's
by Jim Baker.

Mike and Pat sleep on the top
and Jerry and I on the bottom.
I am lucky, Jerry is small.

A lightning bolt came out
of a socket near Pat's elbow.
Even our beds aren't safe.

We have straw ticks
from the ranch.
Grandma reminds us
our guardian angels
are still with us.

The water in the well
has too much sulfur
for drinking or cooking.
We wash clothes, dishes
and ourselves in it.

There is a red hand-pump
by the kitchen sink,
drinking water is hauled
to a tank in the cellar.
When we run out.
there is a milk can with a dipper.

The outhouse,
north of the house.
seems farther away
with winter builds snowdrifts.
Lime doesn't keep it
from smelling bad.
P.S. it is not funny.

There are no trees,
but there are caraganas
around the garden.
Grasshoppers eat the leaves.

The meadowlarks
lay spotted eggs
in grassy dishes
on the prairie.
Robins sing
and bluebirds too.

The Sweet Grass Hills
are thirty-five miles to the east,
like a painting framed
by our front windows.

Friends

My brother Pat
is my best friend
except when Bill,
our cousin, visits
and I am left out.

Eloise and Peggy are friends.
They go to school in town.
Joyce is a girl my age.
Her father works in the oilfield.
She lives in a tar-papered shack
much worse than our house
and wears baggy dresses sewn
from flour sacks.

The Wiley kids
from Oklahoma
are bigger than us.
They are kind, and teach us
about playing softball.

We visit the Birdrattler children
in their tipi
during summer encampments.
We understand each other
even if we have to make sign.

Our very best friend is Blackie.
He makes us laugh,
and keeps us company every day.

Our father, Patrick T. Buckley, at Kennedy Creek

Daddy

He cuts out perfect animals
with a rusty pair of scissors.
He doesn't draw them first.

In the sheep camps
he carved bone
into a tiny buffalo skull
for his best girl.

He loves the girl he married
but with the ranch gone,
he fears losing her too,
and drinks to feel better.

When it is my turn
to go with him
in the 1939 Dodge truck,
I am so excited.
We are going all the way
to Browning to deliver gas.

It is a warm summer day
and the scent of sweet clover
blows in the open windows.
He whistles through his teeth
and promises to teach me how.

Near Blackfeet,
a front wheel breaks
off the truck,
the tanker of gas
too heavy for its frame.
The axle digs into the pavement
and could have caught on fire.
I am not afraid.
I am with him.

Separated

Men sit around our kitchen table,
stories circling fast as the fly wheel
in the engine house.
Men battle the world in overalls.
When they lose,
they laugh at themselves.

I pour coffee
from the black pot
I can hardly lift to be near them.

The living room
where women sit
is full of recipes
and new babies.

Molly has bruises
the colors of pansies
on her round, pretty face.
I don't hear anyone
ask about it,
because they won't.
Some people get mean
when they drink.

I hear Mary mention
how she asks her husband
for money or to drive to town.

My mother doesn't ask Daddy.
She handles the money
and goes when she wants.

We have the old neighbors
we had on the ranch—
Farboes, Sutas, Byes, Baileys,
Kruegers, Bakers, Swensons,
Losings, Bunyaks, Farrs,
Tibbets, McAltpines,
Kellehers, Dyes, Simms
and Hendrix.
We also have the oilfield people.

The Apple Crate

My library is a 1930 Essex,
dark green with cream velvet seats.
Daddy bought it for $25.00
thinking he could make it run.
Yellow tangles of buffalo peas
climb up its hood and tires.

I lean back to admire my books
lined up in an apple crate—
Heidi, The Prince and the Pauper,
Lamb's Shakespeare, Nancy Drew—
And even more.

Willie Suta bought the car,
and I cried over those velvet seats
in my secret place
with my apple crate.
The next secret place I find
is within myself.

The Ranch

Blarney Castle Ranch
is where we used to live.
It was built by my grandfather.

Our family raised sheep
and horses
from 1887 to 1937.
Annie's twelve-room house
stood in a grand circle
of shady cottonwood trees.
There were red ranch buildings.

Buckley Family Ranch, 1887-1937

There was a schoolroom
and a private teacher
for our father's generation,
a gardener and a cook.

The verandah was the place
to hear Grandpa's stories
in the summer,
to play hide-and-seek
and hear the curlews cry.

Our smaller house
had its own yard,
stone benches,
and French windows
for Mama.

We were the last grandchildren
to live there.
We didn't have to worry
like we do now.

We left the ranch for good
on a Sunday morning
after the bank foreclosed
for fifteen thousand dollars,
wouldn't wait for the sheep
to be shipped in the Fall.

There was no time
to say goodbye
to the bum lambs,
to climb one more time
to our cave in the sand rocks.

The sheep dogs
have forgotten us,
and Silver the horse
was sent to the glue factory.
I wish Pat hadn't told me that.

Living in the Past

Our second cousin Kitty
says my parents
would do better
if they forget the past.

I think Dad
took a job
that he is too good for
because this oilfield
is next to the old ranch.

Mama talks about
San Francisco
and the life she shared
with her friend, Maxine.

Border Oilfield Refinery

They were telephone operators
on the President Line
that cruised from Los Angeles
to Vancouver.

She married Daddy,
the son of a rancher,
only to find herself
soaking oily coveralls
in a bucket of gasoline.

When the Blackbirds Come

Making a home out
of a former garage
might have sent her
to Warm Springs
where Montana women
go when the howling winds
and endless work
make them crazy.

Mama finds beauty
in forty quarts of apricots
glistening like baby suns
in sparkling jars.

Even baby suns
cannot hold back
her darkness.

She is in bed the next day
and the next.
Depression has pinned her flat
as the silken blackbirds
flying around the hem
of her favorite 1920's dress.

When she leaves the bedroom,
she is wearing
her good powder blue suit.
A matching turban is tied
over her dark hair,
and a suitcase
is at her feet.

She tells me she is going
with Maxine to rest.
Resting is all
she has been doing
but I don't dare say that.

They will go shopping
and eat in restaurants
Maxine makes her happy.
P.S. Mama, please come home.

Franklin and the Terraplane

Someone new has come to us.
He is nineteen with red hair.
He is Franklin in a Terraplane.

He tells us Oklahoma stories.
We learn to call him
Golly Bum.
It is his favorite expression.

He works on Juedemans' farm
for fifty dollars a month.
Yesterday he invited us kids
for a drive to town
after work.

He took us to Bill's Bar
for hamburgers
and milkshakes in tall glasses.
He bought us tickets
for the show
across the street,
Snow White and the Seven Dwarves.

During the sad parts
Franklin cried like a baby.
We patted him on the back.
We all felt so happy
out in the moonlight
like grownups.

Dear Diary

June 15, 1941

For my tenth birthday
I got a diary
and a pair of anklets.
Eloise gave me
a sterling silver spoon.
Mama baked a cake
with pink candles.

May made another
with green icing
to match my eyes.
I never dreamed
of two cakes
especially for me.

I was born on Flag Day,
and that is special too.

The Radio

We have two stations
on the radio.
One is from Great Falls.
The other is Lethbridge.

After supper, we play outside
when the dishes are done.
We listen to radio programs
on certain nights.

Our favorites are
Fibber McGee and Molly,
The Lone Ranger
and *The Shadow.*

Sometimes we have to leave on a light
after listening to *Inner Sanctum.*
It is very scary.

When I dust the house
in the afternoon
I listen to *Songs of the Prairie*
from Lethbridge.
I sing along with the radio
and do not feel so lonely.

Our Sheepherder

When Old Dave
is not at a sheep outfit,
he is here with us.
When Mama is gone,
he braids my hair
and it smells like bacon grease.

He eats the leftovers
from our plates
making me think
he has been hungry.

Dave Wiley, sheepherder, family friend

He likes a shot
of Three Feathers
when he can get it.
He chews Copenhagen,
lifting a stove lid
to spit next to the cooking.

In forty-below weather
he stands on the porch,
long underwear flapping,
to check the weather.

He spent a year
building a model gold mine
from scrap wood.
He suspended it
in the bunk house
to entertain us kids.

He waits on the hill
to meet us after school
and says, "What happened
to The Buckley family
would wring tears out of a rock."

May

She wears bright dresses,
has short, dark hair
and a big smile.
She is young
and the prettiest girl.

She invites me to visit her
when I am on a walk
in the afternoon
when Mama is asleep.

May's tar-papered shack
is down on the corner
of the main road
to town.

It is so attractive,
with warm orange drapes
and a velvet tapestry
of a leopard
with shimmery spots
and glittering eyes.

She fixes me red Kool-Aid
in a pretty glass and shows me
her jewelry.
Her kindness feels soft
and warm as baby yarn.

My middle name is Mae.
It is a form of Mary,
and I hope I grow up
to be as nice as May.

She was a lady of the night
when Fred met her.
I am not supposed to know
what that means, but I do.

Main Street, Sweet Grass, Montana, 1930s

Sweet Grass

Sweet Grass has two grocery stores,
two restaurants,
Jenny Kirkaboo's Dry goods,
and Webster's Newsstand.
It has a post office, a school,
and many bars.

I don't like the drunks
on the street,
and I wish I didn't feel shy
when people talk to me.

A fat old man
is pretending to be good.
He likes to get little girls alone.
I never want to see him again.

A mean boy named Bobby
took my pearl-handled jack knife.
I loved my jack knife.
I am thinking how to get it back.

I like to go to Jenny's store
to look at the pretty clothes.
She asks me to stay for lunch
while I wait for Daddy.
We have cream of mushroom soup,
and she ties a purple plaid ribbon
in my hair.

Fall is When Summer Dies

Our mother, Dorothy Aman Buckley

Something Nice to Look At

An afternoon drive to Shelby
to look in the stores—
Ben Franklin's and J.C. Penney—
is the highlight of Mama's week.

Twice a year she goes
to Lethbridge or Great Falls,
drives down streets
with shade trees,
lawns and flower beds.
She lets us ride on the trolley
in Lethbridge.

Her smile mirrors her delight
at seeing new fashions
in The Paris or Eaton's.

At home she will make over
an old blue suit with the drape
and buttons of a new one.

Snapshots

Mama chooses snapshots
taken with her Brownie,
using tints and brushes
to transform pale cheeks to rosy,
to streak our hair with gold.

The garden is drying up
and the prairie is parched brown.
Her prairie hills are glowing
with Irish green.

There are oil derricks
and pump jacks
in our photos.
Blackie and the cat
are near us.

Mama's smile is wide
beneath a white beret.
Her pastel children
are free of dust,
prettified in the snaps
sent to her Chicago brother.

No Elegant Pudding

In this unhandy kitchen
you hunt for places
to set things,
the kitchen table or a bench.

Grandma's kitchen
had places for everything,
an oak pie safe
and a long work table
for the day's baking
cooling under blue-striped cloths.

A crystal stand
for the Christmas pudding
sat on the linen tablecloth.
The pudding flamed
in blue and orange
on Christmas Day.

No plum pudding
in the oilfield.
The cake stand is gone,
fought over by women
at the auction sale.

Mother on a Ladder

When she feels good,
she can do anything.
She gave Dad a look
when he wouldn't ask
Mr. Banana for paint.
She isn't afraid to ask,
or to climb the wooden ladder
to scrape and paint outside walls.

The paint gleamed
like whipped butter.
We took turns stirring.
She took up a big brush,
climbed close to the roof
and went to work.

When she moved the ladder,
we helped, and she painted on.
I warmed lima beans and ham
knowing she would not stop.

She made that house
something more
than an oilfield shack.
It looked smug
in its sunny color
with red trim.

Doing the Dishes

I pull out the silverware
with pliers and a pot holder
when the cook stove
heats the water to boiling.
I slide the dishpan to the reservoir
to cool.

The cast iron skillet
is thick with cold grease,
and the potato pan is scorched.
They don't get better,
even with extra
Fels-Naptha flakes
and a copper chore girl
that smells bad.

I can't bear those pans
a moment longer.
I shove them under the stove
to soak until tomorrow.

Oilfield School

I love school.
National Geographic has photos
of places I dream about.
Brown people wear blue tattoos.
They live on the island of Ponope
in the Pacific Ocean.
They are part of a world
I want to see.

Photo 8, Oilfield School; Lower Grades l. to r., Eldon Bye,
Katie Bell Baker, Bertha Swenson, Joyce Wiggins, Pat Buckley,
Teddy Suta, Bonnie Buckley, Eloise Webster (visitor), Mike Buckley

Helping the smaller kids
sound out words
is easy for me.
I encourage Mike
to forget that Miss Hiely
is forcing him
to stop writing
neat little letters
with his left hand.
He has to use his right.
It is terrible for him
and makes him worry
that he won't be able to write
at all.

We take turns cleaning
the school and outhouses.
The outhouses smell terrible
and have spiders.

There are swings to play on,
and I go flying every day.
There is a teeter-totter
and we play tag and have races.

I trade my jelly sandwich
for one of bear meat from Jack Pitman.
He is mean and the meat is tough
and I am sad, thinking of the bear.

Being Told

Why would a grownup
want to tell a child
what could only
make her feel bad?

He stood on the top step,
making him even taller.
I was pinned
to the bottom
stair by his words.
"She will pull out of here
one day, and she won't come back."

What did he know
about Mama?
She might kill herself first.
He didn't know that.
I hate the way his mouth
said the words.
My stomach hurt.
I did not cry.

The Silver Streak

A four-cylinder 1928 Chevrolet
had a wooden box in the back
for groceries.

We wanted to ride in the box
but Mama wouldn't let us.
it could only go to Sweet Grass,
and the little kids
sat on our laps.

The gearshift is topped with a marble
of red, orange and white.
My mother is laughing
at the fate of a flapper
with a trunk of lovely dresses
and a Silver Streak full of kids.

The County Nurse

She is making her yearly visit.
Teacher reminds us
to wash behind our ears.

We may be dusty
but we are not dirty.
Once a week
most of us
are lined up
at the tin wash tub.

Tonight we are scrubbing
ears, necks, hands
and anything else
that needs it.
I make sure the little kids
will pass inspection.

Most of us have some dirt
under raggedy fingernails,
and Pat has oil and grease.

Our ears are clean,
but the nurse flunked the catalogs,
ordering toilet paper
for the outhouses.

The dipper on the milk can
has to go. We will have
pointy little paper water cups,
little cones in a dispenser.

She said the gaslights
gave out dangerous fumes.
School District Number Three
must install electricity.

I fail the eye test.
I am near-sighted, and know now
why I can't read the blackboard well.
I will go to the eye doctor
when there is enough money.
My glasses are on a list with a spare tire.

My Room

I am going to have my own room.
It is the eight-by-five storeroom,
someday bathroom,
but it has a window and it has a door.
I get it because I am the only girl.

Mama makes white curtains
for the window and a vanity
from two orange crates
turned on end with a board
hidden with a dresser scarf
and fabric tacked around
for a pretty skirt.

My bed is an army cot.
My apple crate has a new place,
and I have a room of my own.

Pat and School

I don't understand
why Miss Hiely can't teach
Pat to read.
I know he is smart.
Why can't he read
like I do?
Why does he write 'was'
instead of 'saw'?

He builds intricate machines
with his Mechano set.
He remembers everything
he hears, and is never lazy.

Miss Hiely hit him
on the head
when he couldn't read
a simple sentence.
On the second swing,
she missed and broke the globe.

We don't get hit at home,
so we shouldn't at school.
We never take our troubles
at home to school,
and tell only good things
from school
around the table at supper.

The nuns in Catechism
say that impatience is a sin.
I hate Teacher's meanness
even if we are the only ones
she invites to visit
her cabin at Flathead Lake.

My Apron Went to the Fair

I watched the cars go by
taking kids to the Marias Fair.
From May's house
I counted seven cars,
all with kids.
We cannot go because
it costs too much.

Mama says not to feel bad.
It's just a bunch of animals
like we used to have,
the canned goods
and needlework
no better than ours.

My apron with orange flowers
did go to the fair.
It won third place.
The ribbon is red.

The Cake

I wanted to bake a birthday cake,
but no eggs.

Mrs. Tibbets walked four miles
from her dugout on a hillside.
She had a dozen eggs to sell
for twenty-five cents.

We could not find a quarter
so she walked the eggs back home.

No cake for Mike's eighth birthday.
I read him the story, "The Circus Goat,"
picked wild flowers and put them
by his plate.

The Longest Season

Annie Tennant Buckley

Grandma has come to visit.
She wears a dark print dress,
a hat and veil.
Her brooch is of gold nuggets
on a little spade
from the Alaska Gold Rush.
Grandma's hair is white
and up in a bun.
She is old and beautiful.
Her eyes are blue
as Wedgewood.

She stands very straight,
with her head high.
I am practicing
holding myself like her
even if I do have scoliosis
and have to wear a lift
on ugly brown shoes.

She leads Grace.
Bless Us Oh Lord for these thine gifts...
Everyone's elbows
are off the table.
Pleases can be heard
as food is passed.
There is fried chicken
for supper.

She treats us with dignity.
Each of us has to tell her
something we learned
at school this summer.

She pins scapular medals
on our undershirts
so we will go straight to heaven
if we die in an accident.
She must suspect how dangerous
life is here,
She just doesn't know how much.

Annie Tennant Buckley, paternal grandmother

Looking Good

We go to church
and people tell us
how nice we look
and how happy they are
that we are doing well.

No one knows how hard
it is for us to find something
to wear other than overalls
and my brown knitted dress.

Mama unravels old sweaters,
winding the yarn
in balls for new clothes
like the dreary dress
I should not hate
because she made it.

Where does she get this stuff?
Mike has a white suit
with short pants.
We don't tell him
he looks like a big baby.
Pat says he is lucky
he missed that sissy outfit.

My good dress is navy blue
with a belt.
I wish it could be red plaid.
My underwear
is store-bought,
not made from flour sacks.

Daddy doesn't come often to church,
but he kneels every night
to say his prayers.
He doesn't have to dress up
to do that.

Going to church

Pat Inside an Oil Tank

Everything on this place
smells like gas or oil.
The earth turns black
as a cast-iron griddle,
and Pat's fingernails
are lined with grease
that even Lava soap
won't remove.

He is oiling the wells
and filling barrels
and trucks with gas
when Daddy is gone.

He doesn't get paid
to work on this lease
because he is a kid.
He writes his time
in the time book,
and Mr. Banana
says any money he earns
will be applied to the gasoline
Mama uses in the car.

Home is Like This

Worry here wouldn't fit
in a horse trough—
Too little money
and too many bills.

Daddy's check
is never enough.
Mama paints tablecloths
to sell, but people
can't afford them.

Bonnie, Pat and best friends

She speaks of suicide
in front of Pat and me.
We know what it means
but the little kids don't.

Daddy gets drunk,
but not in front of us.
I love him no matter
what he does.
It is not his fault.

Mama fights with him
about hiding whiskey
in gopher holes.
I have never found any,
so I think she is wrong.

There is something worse.
They told us Blackie ran away.
He wouldn't because he loves us.
Then we heard the truth.
He was smashed
by a falling timber
at the refinery.
I cannot write more.
Oh, Blackie,
we can't get along without you!

Pearl Harbor

December 7, 1941

President Roosevelt made a speech
on the radio.
We are at war with the Japanese.
They bombed Pearl Harbor
and killed many Americans.
Daddy says it will be worse
than World War I when Americans
were gassed in France.

Mama is crying.
She has a brother in the Navy.
No one knows what will happen next.
We looked at a map in an atlas
to see where Hawaii is.
It is a long way from Montana.
It feels like the war is very close.

Pearl Harbor Commemorative Pin

Lessons

Beth comes to visit.
While Mama makes tea,
Beth asks me,
"Who is the most important
person in your life?"

I don't know how to answer.
"My family," I finally reply.
Beth shakes her head.
"No," she says,
"You are."

I never feel important
except when I can help
someone read at school,
and see them understand
something new.

Beth writes poems
about her life with animals
on the Montana prairie.

I write poems too.
She is the first person
I show "Lincoln's Mother"
and she says it is good.
It is written in my diary.

She lives alone
since Mr. Volbrecht died.
It turns out she wasn't married
because he never divorced
his first wife.

"Anything can happen
when you marry a cowboy,"
Mama says.
Well, she ought to know
except a rancher
is not exactly a cowboy.

The Color of Hope

When I was five,
my father drew a sheep
on a piece of muslin.
I embroidered it in crooked red.
"Red work," says Grandma.

Today the sheen of a rayon skein
is radiant as orange mallow
in summer.

Wooden embroidery hoops,
holding stiff muslin,
offer solace from eerie winds,
frosted window panes
and endless days of work.

All across the prairie
snowbound women and girls
take up their hoops
and watch the flowers bloom.
They are messages of hope.

A Special Gift

Mama closes the door
to the living room
a week before Christmas.
She tells us we cannot open it
until Christmas Eve.

Ninety-eight pounds
of sheer will power
rips away torn linoleum
and scrapes black gum
from the rough pine floor.
It is sanded and stained.

She knows so many ways
to make Christmas special,
even though she says
it is a depressing time for her.

We can hardly sleep,
wondering what we will find
on Christmas Eve.

She cooks roast beef
with mashed potatoes and gravy
for supper.
There is mince pie for dessert.
She then opens the door.
We see a room of magic.

There is a tall pine
from the Sweet Grass Hills
blazing with colored bulbs,
and blown glass fruits
brought from San Francisco.

The floor glows warmly
and there are presents
under the tree,
wrapped in white paper,
each tied with red yarn.

My present is a new doll
with dark hair.
I think I am getting too old
to play with dolls,
but she can sit on my bed.
Pat's is a nice leather belt,
Mike's a wooden toy truck,
and Jerry loves his, a toy pistol
in a holster on a belt
with colored stones.

We each get a silver dollar
from Dave, our first.
We give him a box of Copenhagen.
There is a box of candy
from Uncle Johnnie,
and a subscription to *Life* magazine.

Our gifts to Mama and Daddy
are watercolors
of scenes from the mountains.
The frames are molded
from salt and flour
and painted gold.

Daddy's gift to Mama
is a pink silk handkerchief
that says, *From your loving husband.*

Library in Winter

I love the school library.
It has a tall grey cabinet
with five big shelves
full of books.

Daddy is on the school board
and lets me go to the school
when it is closed
to pick out books.

I struggle through snow
up to the top buckle
on my overshoes.
My eyes sting from the wind,
and my green wool scarf,
tied over my nose and mouth,
makes me itch.

I flick the switch
for the overhead light
in the freezing building
that creaks like ghostly bones.

It is hard to read titles
on a dark afternoon.
The books are old
with musty pages.

I pick out
Anne of Green Gables
to read again,
Call of the Wild,
Oliver Twist
and *The World of Oz.*
They are heavy,
but I can carry them.

I want to read all the library books
before I graduate from eighth grade.
The high school in town
has books I've never seen.

Beth Volbrecht, artist, teacher, poet and homesteader

Hair

I should have found time
to wash my own hair
before walking to Itha's
to return a book for Mama.
Mama is gone again.

It is embarrassing
to visit a nice lady
who takes a look at you,
and asks if you would like
to have your hair washed.

She gently washes it
with flowery soap
and brushes it too.
I am embarrassed,
but she says it is nice
having a little girl visit.

I can't stand the idea
that she felt sorry for me.

Snowed In

The snow keeps falling
until it drifts across
the living room windows,
and we can't see out.

Mama says we have plenty to eat.
There is water in the tank,
and we can bake bread.
It will stay thirty below zero
according to the radio.

The wind is howling
around the house,
and I know it will be days
before we can go outside.
Only Daddy goes to oil-up,
and sometimes Pat.

After dark
there is a knock at the door,
which is unbelievable
in the middle of a blizzard.

It is George Krueger,
half-frozen from walking
the fence line to our house
after sliding his car into the ditch
in the storm.

His feet go into
a basin of cool water,
and then warmer
to prevent frostbite.

We fix him eggs and toast
and hot coffee.
He will sleep on the couch.

Babe will wonder
if he spent the night
on a palette in the beer parlor.
She is expecting a baby.

When the blizzard stops,
he will have to walk
the ten miles home.
There is no tractor
to pull him out.

There will be other blizzards
and other neighbors
will spend the night.
It is part of winter.

When the Crocuses Bloom

A Can of Spam

It comes in a blue can
and on the back is a recipe
for Candied Spam
with pineapple and cloves,
the most elegant thing
a ten-year-old ever cooked.

I measure brown sugar,
lumps and all.
I find a dusty can of whole cloves
in the back of the cupboard.

The Spam bakes nicely
in the blue Majestic Range.
It is so special
I set the table with china plates.

Four happy oilfield kids
enjoy a fancy dinner
and play Monopoly
until everyone is too tired
to worry about our parents
not being home.

The Tin Tub

Saturday we heat
water on the stove
to fill the tin wash tub.
It is on the kitchen floor
in front of the stove.
In goes a bar of soap
and a wash rag.

We take turns
in the tub.
Mama washes our hair
and rinses it
with a white pitcher.

The tub gets fuller
and colder.
Being last is terrible.
Being first is also,
when the water is too hot.

The bedroom is freezing,
and I race into my nightgown,
knowing how Blackie used to feel
when he went out
to bark at the coyotes,
and we forgot to let him in.

In the Kitchen

Sometimes we have
fat hot dogs
boiled with sauerkraut.
They are almost as good
as when we roasted them
on sticks over a campfire
at Little Jerusalem.

When the Watkins man
stops by in time for dinner,
Mama finds the money
to buy vanilla extract
and lemon pudding mix.

When she feels good,
she bakes cookies, pie
or cake.
I am learning to bake
and to make soup.

When she sends me
to the cellar
for a jar of fruit or vegetables
we canned last summer,
I can't say no,
but I wish one of the boys
could go instead.

A green salamander
waits on the dirt floor,
tiny chest puffed,
tongue flicking.
He is a reptile.
He terrifies me.

Putting Up Fruit

Sears and Roebuck Catalog

It comes in Fall and Spring,
enough pages
to entertain us for weeks.

Mama orders us nice things
when she can.
Pat loves his aviator's jacket
with brass propeller buttons.
The leather saved his hide
when he skied into a tangle
of barbed wire.

Mama promises me new shoes
for Easter.
I choose patent leather shoes
with grosgrain bows.

Those beautiful shoes
shine like wet black stones
in Kennedy Creek.

I save those shiny shoes
from gumbo and dirty snow,
by wearing my old ones,
carrying the new ones
to the door of Queen of Angels
on Easter Sunday.

The Great Aunt

Aunt Mary is regal
as a sailing ship.
Her white hair is swept high
with ivory combs,
her back straight.
Daddy says she is prissy.
When she was young,
they called her Polly.

Sent to keep her company,
I sleep on the sun porch
when it is warm enough.
There I can gaze at the stars
from under heavy quilts.

She lets me wind
the grandfather's clock.
It displays the phases of the moon.
She describes her daughters
flying across the prairie
on horseback,
and I dream of being one of them.

I empty her china chamber pot
in the morning.
We eat brown bread
with marmalade.
I watch her crochet pineapples
in perfect rows for a lace tablecloth.

Maybe being an old lady
isn't so bad
if you can have toast and jam
instead of oatmeal,
and time to admire your jewelry,
write names on old photos,
and read and do handwork
whenever you feel like it.

Easter

Easter is a rabbit with purple satin ears
brought out for good like Sunday clothes.
Easter celebrates the Resurrection of Christ.

Spring is purple-striped crocuses
blooming in patches of snow.
Pink candles on a lace cloth
show off Mama's china.
Tiny crystal glasses
hold a sip of wine.

We color eggs,
and each of us has an Easter basket
with candy and a little surprise.
Mine is a shiny gold ring
with a red stone.

We have ham for dinner,
and Mrs. Webster and Eloise
bring an orange and black box
of Constant Comment Tea.
We all have tea after dinner.
It tastes like orange and spice.

We go to Church
in our made-over clothes
that look pretty good.
I iron my own dress.

The priest asks us to pray
for a quick end to the war.
Some of the young men
from Sweet Grass
have enlisted, and we pray
for them too.

The tall altar candles are lit
because it is a High Mass.
Daddy is with us
because all Catholics
must go to church
on Christmas and Easter.

Our house in cold weather

Rationing

Rationing doesn't change much
in the oilfield
where shoes are passed down
and repaired until when nothing fits
you get a new pair.

We help Daddy count ration stamps
for gas and diesel.
Gas costs nine cents a gallon.
Diesel is four cents.

Sugar is something we need
for baking and canning,
and not having much will be hard.
We don't have honey
but we have Log Cabin
Syrup in a cabin can.

And most disgusting
is the plastic bag of margarine
with an evil orange pill to color it.
Nothing could make it fit to eat.

The width of belts and hems
in women's dresses is limited
to two inches to save fabric
for the war.

Daddy has a hearing
before the Rationing Board
for losing 2000 gallons worth
of ration stamps for fuel
delivered to farmers.
The 100-gallon stamps
fell out of his pocket
as he helped Mama paint
under the eaves.
The geese had gobbled
every last stamp.

Celebration

We all have a piece of steak,
not just Daddy.
when Mama's check arrives
for the sale of the cabin
she inherited
in Eagle River, Wisconsin.

We are all happy
about the extra money.
We can buy a good car
that doesn't break down
going to the mountains.
We can pay up the grocery bill.

We might even build a sun porch
or a bathroom,
and we won't have to
go to the outhouse
except to admire Mama's murals.

Daddy looks happier,
and isn't drinking so much.
He won't be drafted
because he has four kids
and we are relieved.
He wants to lease
some land to farm.
We will all help.

A Place

On a stop at Bill's bar
I hear a farmer say,
"Well, it is time to get on
out to the place."

The place might be
a tar paper shack
as poor as can be,
but a place is yours
and what you grow there
is yours too.

I have been afraid
that things would never change
the oilfield.
Now it doesn't matter so much.
I have my books and school
and they take me far away
on most days.

When Mama is gone,
cooking is not so hard for me.
It is what I have to do.

The cat had kittens
and they are snugged
against each other
like furry peapods.

Pat has the ranch stories
preserved like sweet cherries
in his mind.
Mike's focus is on doing well,
and he is.
Jerry dreams of good cowboys,
and he is one of them.

Bonnie has her apple crate
and her poems.

About the Author

Bonnie Buckley Maldonado became a fulltime poet when she retired after more than thirty years as a university professor and administrator at Western New Mexico University. In 1999, she was inducted into the New Mexico Women's Hall of Fame for her community service work. She was named the WILLA Finalist in Poetry by Women Writing the West for *It's Only Raven Laughing, 2012.*

She has written poetry since childhood. In 2011, she was named the Inaugural Poet Laureate of Silver City, New Mexico.

The Secret Lives of Us Kids is her fifth book of poetry. Two of her books, *From the Marias River to the North Pole,* and *Montana, Too* focus on her family's pioneer roots in northern Montana. Her fourth book, *Too Personal for Words,* is her testament to aging with humor. Her work appears in various anthologies including *Montana Women Writers: Geography of the Heart,* edited by Caroline Patterson, Farcountry Press, 2007. She received the Best Woman Writer award at the 2008 High Plains Book Festival in Billings, Montana.

Maldonado lives near Pinos Altos, New Mexico, with her husband, Librado and a cadre of adopted pets. Her website is www.bonniebuckleymaldonado.com. Books may be ordered through the website, or in local bookstores. Her email is: bonniemusing@gmail.com. Her mailing address is 23 Oxbow Drive, Silver City, NM 88061

Collaborator, Patrick F. Buckley would rather tell a story than eat. He is an oral historian, oilfield contractor, junkman and collector. His stories and antique drilling equipment are among his favorite collections. Many elements of them are contained in this memoir, including the cars that passed through family hands.

He resides on Buckley Ranch Road, seven miles west of Sweet Grass. His first collaboration with his sister Bonnie was From the *Marias River to the North Pole,* Sweetgrass Books, Farcountry Press, 2006. He may be contacted at Post Office Box 4, Sweet Grass, Montana 59484 or phone, 406 937 3361.